SECRETS YOU'RE NOT SUPPOSED TO KNOW

INTELLIGENCE AGENCIES

Life in the Shadows

Ellis Roxbur...

Published in 2019 by
Lucent Press, an Imprint of Greenhaven Publishing, LLC
353 3rd Avenue
Suite 255
New York, NY 10010

Copyright © 2019 Brown Bear Books Ltd

All rights reserved. No part of this book may be reproduced in any form without permission in writing from the publisher, except by a reviewer.

For Brown Bear Books Ltd:
Managing Editor: Tim Cooke
Designer: Lynne Lennon
Children's Publisher: Anne O'Daly
Design Manager: Keith Davis
Editorial Director: Lindsey Lowe
Picture Manager: Sophie Mortimer

Picture Credits
t=top, c=center, b=bottom, l=left, r=right
Interior: Alamy: dpa/Edgar Bauer, 24; AP: Louis Lanzano, 9; Getty Images: 18, AFP, 25, Ben Birchall, 35, Newsmakers/David Burnett, 7; iStock: Alina555, 36, Peopleimages, 34; Library of Congress: 23; Public Domain: Blackwater, 44, fbi.gov, 4, Jim Garamone, 27, mi5.gov, 17, Ministry of Defence, 19, National Weather Service, 13, Laurie Nevay, 8, Office of United States Senator Dan Coats, 11, whitehouse.gov, 1, 28, 39; Reuters: Eric Gaillard, 5t, Mahmoud Hebbo, 5cr, Jorge Dan Lopez, 12; Robert Hunt Library: 20; Shutterstock: Aleoks, 21, Carlos Caetano, 26, catwalker, 16, Rob Crandall, 40, dejan_k, 33, Kellie L. Folkerts, 37, Nicole S. Glass, 42, Sarah Hipwell, 15, Orlock, 29, Mark Reinstein, 41, Oleh Slepchenko, 43, Ken Tannenbaum, 10, turtix, 45; US Department of Defense: Gino Reyes, 31; US Department of State: 32.
Front cover: (background) Carolyn Cole/Getty Images; (foreground) Aude Guerrucci-Pool/Getty Images.

Brown Bear Books has made every attempt to contact the copyright holder.
If anyone has any information please contact licensing@brownbearbooks.co.uk

Cataloging-in-Publication Data

Names: Roxburgh, Ellis.
Title: Intelligence agencies: life in the shadows / Ellis Roxburgh.
Description: New York : Lucent Press, 2019. | Series: Classified: secrets you're not supposed to know | Includes glossary and index.
Identifiers: ISBN 9781534564381 (pbk.) | ISBN 9781534564367 (library bound)
Subjects: LCSH: Spies--Juvenile literature. | Intelligence service--Juvenile literature. | Espionage--Juvenile literature.
Classification: LCC JF1525.I6 R69 2019 | DDC 327.12--dc23

Manufactured in the United States of America

CPSIA Compliance Information: Batch #BS18KL
For further information contact Rosen Publishing, New York, New York at 1-800-237-9932

CONTENTS

Gathering Information 4

What Are Intelligence Agencies? 6

Meet the Spies 14

Propaganda and Deception 22

Monitoring Threats 30

Intelligence Agencies and
   Government 38

Glossary 46

Further Resources 47

Index 48

GATHERING INFORMATION

In its government meaning, intelligence refers to the collection of information that has military or political value. The information comes from many sources.

Intelligence agencies are government bodies whose chief task is to gather and analyze intelligence to support government operations. At home, these agencies usually carry out activities relating to threats to national security and issues of law enforcement. Away from home, intelligence agencies gather information in other countries that might be useful for planning foreign policy or military operations.

>> **Agents at Work** The Federal Bureau of Investigation (FBI) is the main U.S. domestic intelligence agency.

>> On Watch
Intelligence agencies often monitor people's movements to detect crime.

>> Syrian Fighters
Intelligence agencies might become involved in conflict in other countries.

RANGE OF DUTIES

Intelligence agencies might warn people to be aware of a heightened threat of terrorist attacks, for example. They might advise the government about potentially hostile actions by another country, or detect breeches of national security by spies. A more controversial activity is helping to influence the behavior of other countries, perhaps by using **propaganda**. Another duty is defensive. Intelligence agencies protect national security against intrusion by the intelligence agencies of foreign powers. This protection is known as **counterintelligence**.

WHAT ARE INTELLIGENCE AGENCIES?

There are many types of intelligence agencies. Most are defined by the kind of information they collect, although they usually operate in similar ways.

The activities undertaken by intelligence agencies can be either overt, meaning open, or covert, meaning hidden. The public rarely learns of covert operations, unless their existence is somehow revealed. The intelligence that agencies gather can also be overt or covert. Overt information is widely available. It includes sources such as press reports, financial statistics, travel records, and so on. Covert information is gathered without people's knowledge. It is gathered by means such as **espionage** or through intercepting people's private communications by tapping their phones or emails. Or it is collected by carrying out **surveillance** using satellite cameras or high-altitude **unmanned aerial vehicles** (UAVs), or drones.

CLASSIFIED

>> **Langley, Virginia**
Agents meet at the headquarters of the Central Intelligence Agency (CIA), the leading U.S. overseas intelligence agency.

FAST FACTS

HOME AND ABROAD
Virtually all countries have at least one intelligence agency to assist with national security. Most also have an overseas agency to gather information useful to the country. This can be done openly from public sources or secretly by using espionage and spies.

NATIONAL AND FOREIGN

Many countries have separate agencies to deal with national intelligence and with foreign intelligence. In the United Kingdom, Military Intelligence, Section 5 (known as MI5) is responsible for **domestic** security and counter-intelligence. MI6, the Secret Intelligence Service, works secretly abroad to gather political and economic information. In France, domestic intelligence is the responsibility of the General Directorate for Internal Security (GDSI). Foreign intelligence is handled by the General Directorate for External Security (DGSE).

>> **On Display** MI6 is based in a prominent building on the Thames River in London.

In the United States, the Federal Bureau of Investigation (FBI) is the best-known domestic intelligence and law-enforcement agency. The Central Intelligence Agency (CIA) is responsible for gathering information abroad and trying to influence events in foreign countries. In the past, the CIA has been involved in schemes to **assassinate** or depose foreign leaders. The agency has also sent money to political movements challenging governments it sees as threatening U.S. interests.

>> **Desk Jobs** FBI agents spend a lot of time using computers to track criminal activity.

WHAT DO YOU THINK?

In the past, the CIA has been accused of interfering with the affairs of other countries. This is against international law. In 1980s, for example, the CIA sent funds to right-wing Contra rebels in Nicaragua. The Contras were fighting to overthrow the elected Sandinista government. The CIA judged Sandinista policies to be harmful to U.S. economic interests in Nicaragua. Does that justify its involvement in Nicaragua's civil war?

>> **Terror Attacks** On September 11, 2001, terrorists flew planes into the World Trade Center. They also attacked the Pentagon in Washington, D.C.

COORDINATING ROLE

The Office of the Director of National Intelligence was created after U.S. intelligence failed to predict the terrorist attacks of 9/11 in 2001. Critics argued that the different U.S. intelligence agencies had not shared crucial information among themselves. The Director of National Intelligence is tasked with making sure the operations of all agencies are coordinated.

The FBI and CIA are just the two best known of 17 U.S. intelligence agencies, which in 2015 had a combined budget of over $66 billion. The head of the intelligence community, and also senior intelligence advisor to the U.S. government, is the Director of National Intelligence.

The director's office was created to coordinate the work of the various intelligence agencies. It created Intelligence Advanced Resarch Projects Activity (IARPA) to coordinate their efforts better.

A LARGE AGENCY

The National Security Agency (NSA) mainly monitors and collects data from electronic communications. It was once so secret that NSA was said to stand for "No such agency." The NSA uses cutting-edge technology, **codebreakers**, and mathematicians to carry out controversial large-scale surveillance programs of American citizens.

>> **Leader** Dan Coats became Director of National Intelligence in 2017.

CONFLICT AND CRIME

The Defense Intelligence Agency is part of the U.S. military **establishment**. It gathers intelligence about foreign armies, which is used in the event of a possible conflict. The Bureau of Intelligence and Research, meanwhile, is part of the Department of State. It analyzes information on global affairs and warns about developments such as drug smuggling or human trafficking that might threaten U.S. foreign policy objectives in particular parts of the world.

FOR AND AGAINST

The NSA carries out large-scale surveillance of U.S. citizens. Analysts say this is necessary to prevent terrorist plots or criminal activity before they happen. Critics say it is an invasion of personal privacy. Do you think increased security justifies a loss of privacy?

FIGHTING CRIME

The Office of National Security Intelligence is part of the Drug Enforcement Administration (DEA). It gives DEA agents information to help them investigate and prosecute drug dealers. The Department of the Treasury has its own Office of Intelligence and Analysis. One of its main duties is to prevent criminals hiding or **laundering** money in the United States.

>> **Drug Bust**
CIA operatives in Latin America intercept a shipment of drugs headed to the United States.

>> **Natural Disaster** Intelligence agencies warn of threats such as Hurricane Ivan, which hit the Caribbean and southern United States in 2004.

In the Department of Energy, the Office of Intelligence and Counterintelligence grew out of efforts in the 1950s to spy on the Soviet atomic bomb program. It provides information on foreign nuclear powers and on **energy security**. The National Geospatial-Intelligence Agency provides analysis of the Earth's natural and human-made features to the Defense Department for use during wars but also for disaster relief. Disaster relief is also an important task of the satellites built and operated by the National Reconnaissance Office, which also uses satellite imagery to identify terrorist activity in peacetime or military operations during wartime.

All branches of the U.S. military—Air Force, Army, Navy, and Marine Corps—plus the Coast Guard also have their own intelligence agencies.

MEET THE SPIES

One of the best-known roles of intelligence agencies is to organize espionage. Espionage gathers information from sources that are hidden or not.

A lot of what spies do is secret, but most espionage services operate in a similar way. Professional intelligence agents recruit assets, who are people who gather information for them. Often, agents deliberately approach assets with access to particular information—say, someone who works in a military planning office. At other times, they groom recruits so they can apply for particular jobs. It is the agent's job to manage a range of assets and to judge the usefulness of the information they supply. Agents also gather information from broader sources, such as foreign media and official radio and TV stations. Cyber-espionage now plays a major role in spying activites. It involves **hacking** into the computer systems of governments and agencies. While the details spies discover are of little significance on their own, experienced agents can put them together to reveal a far more important picture about economic or political activities.

CLASSIFIED

>> **Ready to Kill** The popular view of spies is different from the reality, which is less glamorous—but can be just as dangerous.

FAST FACTS

SPY HISTORY

Spies have operated under cover since ancient times, when Roman agents communicated using an alphabetical **cipher**. Some of the most famous spies in history have been women. They include Rose O'Neal Greenhow, who spied for the Confederates during the Civil War (1861–1865), and Mata Hari, a dancer who spied for Germany in World War I (1914–1918).

>> **James Bond** Ian Fleming, author of the James Bond novels, had served as a British naval intelligence officer.

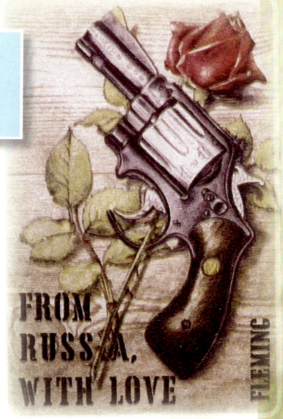

FICTION AND FACT

The word "spy" sometimes suggests a world of glamor and adventure. During the Cold War from 1947 to 1991, the world was divided into political blocs led by the United States and the Soviet Union. Spies became the subject of many novels and adventure movies. James Bond was probably the most famous of these fictional secret agents. He used a combination of cutting-edge technology and a "license to kill" to protect British interests in the world.

In the modern world, spying is less glamorous and usually less risky—but it still yields essential information about the activities of other countries or of criminal or terrorist groups. However, much of the secrecy that once surrounded espionage has disappeared. In the James Bond books, for example, Bond's boss was code-named "M."

PICKING UP FACTS

Many intelligence agents today work almost entirely online. They spend their time monitoring social media sites and visiting chat rooms, usually under an **alias**. They are trying to pick up random tidbits of information about, for example, activity on a military base. If all sports events are cancelled on a certain day, for example, that might reveal that some kind of operation is being planned.

The true identity of the director of MI5 was first revealed in 1992. Since then, their identity has been widely known. In 2009, MI5 placed advertisements in teachers' newspapers seeking to recruit staff. In 2016, it published a puzzle in the press and invited readers to solve it in the hopes of recruiting potential codebreakers.

WORKING ABROAD

Secrecy still surrounds the identity of many people who **illicitly** gather information. Spies often live in foreign countries. Some do so openly, working as intelligence agents within their country's embassy, so the other government is aware of them.

>> **Recruiting** This newspaper ad was placed by MI6 to recruit Somali assets.

FOR AND AGAINST

With so much information available today on the Internet, some intelligence agencies are reducing their reliance on secret agents. Living undercover is risky, and it often happens that spies discover little that is not already known. However, some analysts believe that using human agents is the only way to discover really significant secrets of the enemy.

However, some spies live abroad in secret. In 2010, for example, the FBI arrested 10 Russians living as "deep cover" spies around New York City. They included Richard and Cynthia Murphy, who lived with their two young daughters on a quiet street in Montclair, New Jersey. After watching them for years, the FBI figured out the couple were gathering information for the Russian intelligence agency and passing it on in secret handovers. The couple's real names were Vladimir and Lydia Guryev. Two weeks after their arrests, the Russian spies and their children were sent back to Russia in exchange for four Western spies held there. Despite the Cold War being over, the United States and Russia were still using deep-cover agents.

>> **American Dream**
Cynthia and Richard Murphy enjoy a barbecue in New Jersey.

RIVALS WITH RUSSIA

The rivalry between the United States and Russia grew again during the 2016 U.S. presidential election campaign. After the election, U.S. intelligence agencies accused Russia of trying to influence the vote through its hacking and release of emails related to the Democratic Party. The Russians denied any such interference. In December 2016, President Barack Obama expelled Russian **diplomats** from the United States. In July 2017, Congress voted to punish Russia for its cybercrimes. In response, Russia expelled U.S. diplomats and closed U.S. properties in Russia in retaliation.

>> **Listening In** Many spies now work in agencies such as Britain's Government Communications Headquarters, monitoring global communications.

>> **Mushroom Cloud** The Soviet Union used spies to try to learn how to make atomic bombs like those the United States dropped on Japan in August 1945.

WHAT DO YOU THINK?

During the Cold War, revealing secrets to an enemy country was considered **treason.** It was punishable by death. In 1953, a married American couple named Julius and Ethel Rosenberg were executed for giving U.S. nuclear secrets to the Soviet Union. Today, spies are more often simply thrown out of the country where they work. What punishment do you think should be given to spies?

In summer 2017, the head of U.S. Counterintelligence, William Evanina, said that Russian espionage remained at a high level. He said that spies were hacking government and industry secrets. Although he acknowledged that U.S. agents were active in Russia, he suggested that the Russians had far more spies operating within the United States. The disproportion began during the Cold War. In addition, Evanina identified a change in the type of spies the Russians were using. Rather than relying on intelligence agents, they were also recruiting businessmen, engineers, and other contractors traveling to the United States.

>> **U.S. Embassy** Confidential business is carried out on the top floors of the embassy in Moscow, Russia, to try to keep it secret.

PROPAGANDA AND DECEPTION

Intelligence operations overseas have involved agencies in activies that are barely legal or even outright illegal.

One of the most controversial duties of intelligence agencies is to spread propaganda. This takes different forms, but usually sets out to encourage people in other countries to support the agency's own country or its values, or to turn against other values. Propaganda might take the form of TV or radio broadcasts aimed at people in states such as Syria and Iraq that discourage them from joining the Islamist terror group known as Islamic State in Iraq and Syria, or ISIS. ISIS itself finds recruits by **radicalizing** them using online propaganda, including videos and sermons.

In the past, such activity has been a large part of the work of U.S. intelligence agencies, particularly during times of conflict. In World War II, the Vietnam War, and later conflicts, the different branches of U.S. military intelligence have put great effort into gaining the support of enemy populations and deceiving enemy military forces.

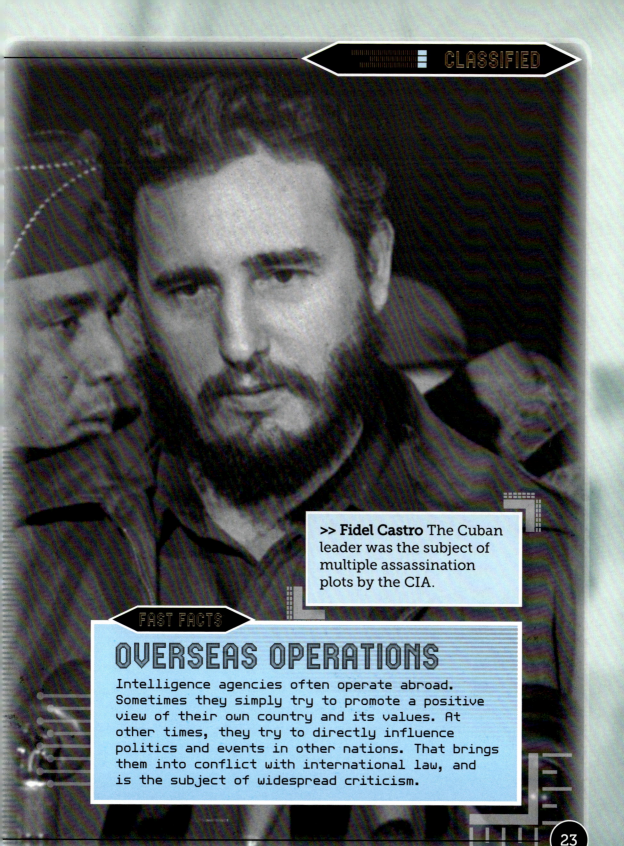

CLASSIFIED

>> **Fidel Castro** The Cuban leader was the subject of multiple assassination plots by the CIA.

FAST FACTS

OVERSEAS OPERATIONS

Intelligence agencies often operate abroad. Sometimes they simply try to promote a positive view of their own country and its values. At other times, they try to directly influence politics and events in other nations. That brings them into conflict with international law, and is the subject of widespread criticism.

>> **Chinese Protests** In 1989, protesters seeking democracy in China learned about events from a U.S. radio station.

VOICE OF AMERICA

The work of intelligence agencies in this area overlaps with that of other government bodies. The radio station Voice of America (VOA), for example, was set up during World War II to broadcast news around the world. Many people see the role of VOA as being to generate positive views of the United States in other countries—in other words, as a form of propaganda. It broadcasts in more than 40 languages.

In 1989, VOA kept Chinese listeners up to date with a pro-democracy movement in China, which was not reported in the local media. VOA later focused on the Middle East, which was destabilized by the conflict in Syria, the rise of ISIS, and clashes between Sunni and Shia Muslims.

FOR AND AGAINST

Voice of America costs U.S. taxpayers $218 million in 2016. Critics say that this money would be better spent on Americans than on broadcasting to foreign countries. However, supporters of VOA argue that it is crucial to promoting U.S. values and interests, particularly in unstable regions of the world. They also claim it is a relatively cheap way of doing so.

FOREIGN INVOLVEMENT

Influencing the affairs of other countries is one of the most controversial tasks of intelligence agencies. Interfering in the work of other governments is against international law. In the 1900s, the CIA tried several times to influence politics in other countries. In 1953, for example, the CIA and UK intelligence organized a **coup** to overthrow the elected government of Iran.

>> **Iranian Rebels** Anti-government protestors ride on a tank in Iran in 1953, during a coup backed by U.S. and UK intelligence.

>> **Wetsuit** One scheme to kill Fidel Castro is said to have involved smearing his wetsuit with poison.

Iranian revolutionaries removed the newly elected prime minister, Mohammad Mossadegh, from office and placed him under **house arrest**. The CIA helped plan and fund the coup, bribing people to take part and issuing propaganda to back the coup. The United States and Great Britain wanted to strengthen the rule of Iran's unelected ruler, the Shah, because they thought he would give their oil companies greater freedom to operate than Mossadegh's government had.

CHANGING ATTITUDES

In the 1960s, the CIA is said to have come up with more than 600 plans to assassinate Fidel Castro, the leader of Cuba. They were said to be suspicious of his close relations with the communist Soviet Union. Many of the plans had little chance of being successful, such as giving him an exploding cigar or lining his wetsuit with poison (he was an enthusiastic scuba diver). Other plans involved stabbing Castro with a poison ballpoint pen or using Mafia **hitmen** to murder him.

Negative public reaction to such covert operations led to more caution in U.S. intelligence activity overseas. In the 1990s, for example, the CIA warned about the growing ability of the terrorist group al-Qaeda to strike at targets inside the United States. Presidents Bill Clinton and George W. Bush did not want to risk a backlash by assassinating the group's leader, Osama bin Laden. In September 2001, al-Qaeda attacked targets in New York City and Washington, D.C., killing nearly 3,000 people.

After the raids, the CIA helped identify al-Qaeda as the terror group responsible. Al-Qaeda was based in Afghanistan, and the CIA began a plan to coordinate Afghan tribespeople against the government sheltering al-Qaeda.

>> **Afghan Allies**
Tribesmen coordinated by the CIA to fight against the Afghan government.

KILLING BIN LADEN

In 2002 the CIA learned that Osama bin Laden was in Pakistan. Agents interrogated al-Qaeda operatives to identify a **courier** who carried messages to bin Laden. They followed the courier to a **compound** in the city of Abbottabad. The CIA monitored the compound until CIA and Navy SEAL forces raided the compound on May 2, 2011, killing bin Laden.

>> **Looking On**
President Obama and his advisors watch the operation to kill Osama bin Laden.

As the United States assembled a **coalition** of nations to invade Afghanistan, where al-Qaeda was based, CIA operatives and U.S. **special forces** worked with Afghan tribespeople. They created what was called the Northern Alliance and fought with its fighters as they targeted strongpoints of al-Qaeda and the Taliban who ran the Afghan government. In the war that followed, the U.S.-led coalition overthrew the Taliban. Bin Laden himself escaped, but 10 years later, the CIA played a leading role in locating and assassinating him.

THE CIA IN SYRIA

In 2012, the CIA became involved in a civil war in Syria. Rebels were fighting the government of President Bashar al-Assad. The CIA helped train and arm rebel fighters, and sent them weapons. The United States was one of a number of countries that originally agreed to fund the rebel Free Syrian Army (FSA). However, as the civil war dragged on, it created a **power vacuum** in Syria. This allowed the ISIS terror group to establish control of large parts of the country. It became clear that the U.S. operation was no longer having the intended outcome.

In summer 2017, President Donald Trump ordered the CIA to scale back its operations inside Syria.

>> **Explosion** Syrian forces attack a rebel base in Syria.

WHAT DO YOU THINK?

In 2017, President Trump identified ISIS as the main U.S. enemy in Syria. He suggested cooperating with Russia and the Syrian government to fight ISIS. Russia and the United States often have conflicting interests. The Syrian government is accused of attacking its own people. Should the United States work with such allies?

MONITORING THREATS

A key role in the job of intelligence agencies is to keep watch for any threats to the nation or its institutions.

Some of those threats may come from outside, such as warfare, cybercrime, or **humanitarian** crises or natural disasters that disrupt normal economic activity or movement of people, goods, or information. Other threats may be internal, or domestic. They might again be linked to crises, but are more commonly linked to organized crime and in particular to terrorism. Intelligence agencies throughout the world have expanded their anti-terrorism activities significantly since the rise of Islamist terrorism from the 1990s. The terrorist attacks of September 11, 2001, in the United States and later attacks in Europe caused a significant increase in anti-terrorism operations.

EXTERNAL THREATS

Intelligence agencies use sources such as monitoring broadcasters and newspapers, analyzing official reports, and espionage to monitor what is happening in other countries.

 CLASSIFIED

>> **Under Watch** A guard watches the U.S. prison at Guantanamo Bay in Cuba, which holds prisoners captured in the war on terrorism.

FAST FACTS

DEFENSIVE ROLE

Defense of the country and its citizens is a major task of all intelligence agencies. Sometimes, this is as simple as assessing risk in order to advise people to avoid trouble in certain countries. At other times, however, it requires the active investigation of possible risks from terrorist or criminal activity.

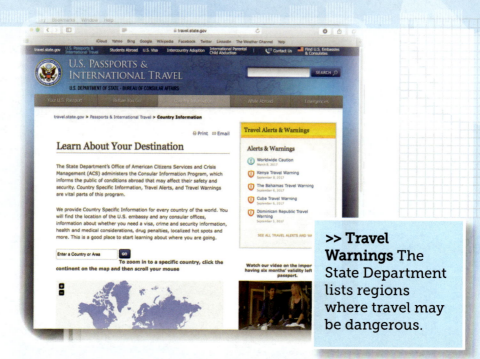

>> Travel Warnings The State Department lists regions where travel may be dangerous.

U.S. agencies figure out the level of threat to Americans or American businesses from warfare or other international emergencies. They can learn about weapons build-ups or troop movements that might suggest imminent military action. If they suspect that a country may be near revolution, they might inform the State Department so that it can advise U.S. businesses to secure their interests or advise American travelers not to visit. In the first half of 2017, for example, the State Department issued travel warnings for about 40 countries. The reasons for issuing warnings ranged from the possibility of warfare or a general threat of terrorism to a specific threat of terrorism targeted against Americans. They also include anticipated natural disasters, such as hurricanes or volcanic eruptions.

As much as possible, intelligence agencies try to predict international issues before they arise. That gives the government time to plan emergency measures, such as the **evacuation** of U.S. citizens or moving military personnel in place.

>> **Attack Site** Terrorists attacked tourists at the temple of Hatshepsut in Egypt in 1997.

CYBERCRIME

Every year, the U.S. intelligence agencies publish a list of the major threats facing U.S. interests around the world. In 2011, the threat of cyber attack appeared on the list for the first time. Since 2013, cyberattack has topped the list every year.

WHAT DO YOU THINK?

One way the CIA has gotten information from captured terrorists is called enhanced interrogation. It uses techniques such as sleep deprivation, confinement in small boxes, and waterboarding, which makes the victim feel as if they are being drowned. It is illegal in the United States because it is classified as torture. However, in the early 2000s it was carried out at U.S. "black sites" around the world, including the U.S. base at Guantanamo Bay in Cuba. Is it justified to use torture to obtain information from terror suspects?

>> **Cybercrime** Criminals or hostile agents can disrupt economic activity and learn national secrets.

Cybercrime takes a number of different forms. In what is termed cyber warfare, hackers working for one country target and disrupt the infrastructure of another country. This happened in 2015, when Russian hackers disrupted power supplies in eastern Ukraine. At the time, Russia and Ukraine were in a fierce dispute over control of the Crimea Peninsula, a part of Ukraine inhabited by many Russians and claimed by Russia. The cyber **sabotage** was part of a conflict that also included armed military clashes.

Another level of cybercrime resembles a form of espionage. Hackers try to infiltrate secure computer systems belonging to other governments in order to learn about their plans and intentions. The hackers aim to do this without being noticed.

Sometimes this type of activity is carried out by groups rather than countries, but it is often also carried out by intelligence agencies. At the same time, intelligence agencies are tasked with protecting their own cyber networks from being hacked.

INTERNAL THREATS

At home, much activity by intelligence agencies is focused on the threat from Islamist terrorism. In the first decades of the 2000s, the United States, Britain, France, Spain, and other countries were attacked by "homegrown" Islamist terrorists. The terrorists were either born in the country they attacked or had lived there for a long time. This makes them more difficult to discover.

>> Monitoring British agents use computers to intercept electronic communications.

FOR AND AGAINST

In 2017, the U.S. government introduced limits on migration from seven mainly Muslim countries: Iraq, Syria, Iran, Libya, Somalia, Sudan, and Yemen. The government argued that the countries exported terrorism. Critics argued that no citizens of the countries had committed terrorist acts against the United States, which are most often carried out by U.S. citizens.

35

>> **Library Books** The PATRIOT Act gave U.S. intelligence agencies powers to monitor people's library habits.

Intelligence agencies try to prevent such attacks. They identify and monitor individuals known to have anti-Western prejudices or who support the idea of terrorism. They use **informants** within Muslim communities to learn of possible attacks.

Because the terrorists are part of the general population, intelligence agencies argue that they have to monitor the popuation more widely. Agencies have acquired wide powers to intercept the communications of potential terrorists.

PATRIOT ACT

The USA PATRIOT Act was passed after the 2001 9/11 terror attacks. It gave intelligence agencies increased powers. For example, it made it legal to detain immigrants indefinitely and to search homes or businesses without the owners' knowledge. It also gave the FBI increased power to search phone, computer, and business records without requiring a court order.

Such agencies might listen to people's private phone calls or read their emails. The USA PATRIOT Act of 2001 gave U.S. intelligence agencies the power to find out what library books people borrowed in case they suggested a person had sympathy with extremist causes.

FIGHTING CRIME

Intelligence agencies also work with law enforcement to be alert for the threat from major crime. This might involve large-scale financial fraud, drug-running, or people-smuggling. Intelligence agencies gather information, act on tip-offs, and use informants to learn about criminal plans. Such information might be useful to the United States Border Patrol in preventing people crossing the borders into the country illegally or to the Drug Enforcement Agency in preventing a major shipment of drugs.

>> **U.S. Border** A fence divides the United States and Mexico. Intelligence agencies warn about attempts to smuggle people into the United States.

Intelligence Agencies and Government

Intelligence agencies are part of the bureaucracy of a country's government. However, they sometimes have a conflicted relationship with politicians.

After the 2016 U.S. presidential election, the major U.S. intelligence agencies announced that they had evidence that Russian hackers had interfered in the election campaign. In particular, the hackers had gotten hold of and released tens of thousands of emails intended to discredit the Democratic Party candidate for president, Hillary Clinton. In addition, the Russians had planted fake news stories on social media sites such as Facebook. In 2017, Congress voted to impose **sanctions** on Russia as a punishment for cybercrimes.

However, not everyone agreed with the intelligence agencies and Congress. The new U.S. president, Donald J. Trump, publicly doubted Russian involvement in the elections.

CLASSIFIED

>> **U.S. Congress**
It can be difficult for the government to oversee the activities of intelligence agencies that operate in secret.

FAST FACTS

NATIONAL STRUCTURE

The U.S. intelligence community includes all the government agencies that carry out intelligence work. It is part of the executive branch of the U.S. government. Its head is the director of National Intelligence, who reports directly to the U.S. president.

>> **2016 Election** Intelligence agencies say Russia interfered in the presidential election, but Donald Trump denied the suggestion.

President Trump also insisted that, even if the Russians were involved in the election, no one involved in his campaign had acted with them or encouraged them. This put the president on a collision course with the intelligence community. As a part of its investigations into Russia's role in the election, the FBI had begun an investigation into the Trump campaign.

The president fired the director of the FBI, a veteran intelligence officer named James Comey. Trump accused Comey of incompetence. Comey said that Trump had asked him to stop investigating his advisor Michael Flynn. This request would have been unlawful, as the Constitution forbids members of the executive arm of government, which includes the president, to interfere in a legal investigation.

SECRETS AND TRANSPARENCY

For many observers, the incident highlighted the potential clash of interests between politicians and the intelligence agencies. In many countries other than the United States, elected politicians are suspicious about intelligence activities such as espionage and covert overseas influence. Politicians in democracies often argue for transparency in all forms of government, but intelligence agencies are secretive and unwilling to reveal their methods or their sources. The agencies say that secrecy is vital in order, for example, to protect the assets who give them information. The assets would not do this if their identity were under threat of being revealed.

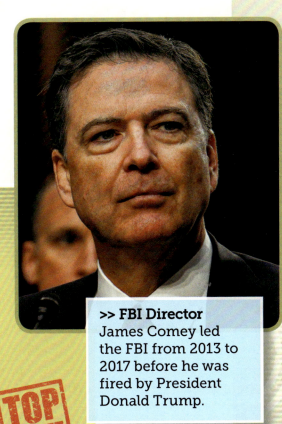

>> **FBI Director** James Comey led the FBI from 2013 to 2017 before he was fired by President Donald Trump.

FIRED

Donald Trump fired James Comey from the FBI because he feared Comey was undermining his government. However, in 2016 it was the Democrats who were complaining about Comey. In the run-up to the presidential election, Comey said the FBI was investigating Democratic candidate Hillary Clinton.

FOR AND AGAINST

In May 2017, special counsel Robert Mueller was appointed to investigate links between the electoral campaign of Donald Trump (below) and groups in Russia. Supporters of the move said that it was necessary to investigate Russian influence on the 2016 election. Trump and his supporters alleged that it was part of an establishment witch hunt against a **populist** president.

Critics of intelligence agencies are also concerned about another aspect of their behavior. Supporters of President Trump frequently complained about the traditional branches of the government. They saw the CIA and the FBI as part of a "deep state." They accused this group of career intelligence agents and government employees of following their own agenda and policy, regardless of the democratically elected politicians in the government. Although Trump supporters were vocal in complaints about the "deep state," Democrats and Republicans have been making similar complaints since World War II.

Both sides regularly allege that the deep state supports the policies of the other party and opposes their own. Most observers suggest that the deep state does not actually exist. Criticism directed toward it is more likely simply an expression of politicians' frustration with agencies whose work is often secretive and whose general focus tends to be on longer-term goals rather than short-term political gains.

HEAVY RESPONSIBILITIES

The existence of the "deep state" conspiracy theory is a reminder that intelligence agencies are not like other arms of government. Their duties require them to operate largely independently and covertly, with relatively limited oversight from elected politicians. Indeed, intelligence agents might even be required to spy on politicians and officials in their own governments who are suspected of wrongdoing.

>> **Deep State**
Do shadowy forces inside government really try to enforce their own agenda on the country?

>> **Private Guards**
Blackwater operatives pose with trainees at a gun range.

WHAT DO YOU THINK?

Blackwater was founded as a private company in 1997. It provides training and security services to U.S. military and law enforcement organizations. Blackwater personnel act as security guards for CIA bases, and have protected U.S. forces in Bosnia and Israel. Despite being a private company, its operatives have been involved in numerous U.S. conflicts, such as the Iraq and Afghanistan wars. Should a company that operates for profit be able to take on roles traditionally limited to a country's official intelligence agencies and armed forces?

SUSPICION AND CONTROVERSY

Those involved in gathering intelligence say that they do it to protect democracy and the Constitution. Their opponents argue that they do so in ways that are nondemocratic and unconstitutional. This has led to a broader suspicion of intelligence agencies. The agencies have access to sensitive private information about citizens and have wide-ranging powers to investigate and detain individuals. For that reason, their work is framed in a robust system of legislation that prevents them from acting as they wish. Simply having to act in a secretive way is no reason for intelligence agencies to operate outside the law. Although the work of intelligence agencies remains vital, it seems that the agencies and their behavior will remain as controversial in the future as they often have been in the past.

>> **U.S. Capitol** Is it ever possible for governments to monitor the work of intelligence agencies?

GLOSSARY

alias A false identity.

assassinate To murder someone for a political reason.

cipher A code in which letters in a message are substituted by other letters.

coalition A temporary alliance of countries to cooperate to achieve a common goal.

codebreakers People who figure out how to read coded messages and ciphers.

compound A secure area surrounded by a fence or wall.

counterintelligence Organized efforts to prevent an enemy gaining information about national security.

coup The overthrow of a government.

courier Someone who delivers packages and messages.

diplomats Officials who represent their country abroad.

domestic Relating to events within a country rather than abroad.

energy security A country's ability to have uninterrupted access to affordable sources of energy.

espionage Using spying or spies to gain political or military information.

establishment A powerful group within society that exercises influence over policy and usually resists change.

evacuation The act of moving someone from a place of danger.

hacking Gaining unauthorized access to a computer system.

hitmen People who are paid to kill someone, usually for a criminal or political organization.

house arrest A form of detention when a person is confined to a residence.

humanitarian Motivated by a desire to improve the welfare of people.

illicitly In a morally unacceptable way.

informants People who give information to authorities, particularly about their family, friends, or colleagues.

laundering Concealing the origins of money gained illegally.

populist A politician who appeals to ordinary people and their concerns.

power vacuum A situation in which no group has authority to impose control.

propaganda Information intended to influence people's way of thinking.

radicalizing Influencing people to hold extreme attitudes.

sabotage To destroy or damage something for political advantage.

sanctions Penalties for disobeying a law, such as restrictions on trade.

special forces Elite troops who carry out small-scale operations.

surveillance The careful watching of a place or an individual.

treason The crime of betraying one's country.

unmanned aerial vehicles Aircraft piloted by onboard computers or by pilots using remote control.

FURTHER RESOURCES

Books

Coddington, Andrew. *Mass Government Surveillance: Spying on Citizens*. Spying, Surveillance, and Privacy in the 21st Century. New York: Cavendish Square Publishing, 2017.

Collard, Sneed B. *The CIA and FBI: Top Secret*. Freedom Forces. Vero Beach, FL: Rourke Publishing Group, 2013.

Curley, Robert. *Spy Agencies, Intelligence Operations, and the People Behind Them*. Intelligence and Counterintelligence. New York: Rosen Publishing, 2013.

Lassieur, Allison. *Cyber Spies and Secret Agents of Modern Times*. Spies! North Mankato, MN: Compass Point Books, 2017.

Streissguth, Tom. *The Security Agencies of the United States: How the CIA, FBI, NSA, and Homeland Security Keep Us Safe*. Constitution and the US Government. Berkeley Heights, NJ: Enslow Publishers, 2012.

Websites

CIA Kids' Page
www.cia.gov/kids-page
An introduction for young readers to the CIA, with games and activities.

Federal Bureau of Investigation
people.howstuffworks.com/fbi.htm
This article from How Stuff Works explains how the FBI fights crime.

IARPA
science.howstuffworks.com/iarpa.htm
A description of Intelligence Advanced Research Projects Activity and how it brings intelligence agencies together.

International Intelligence
encyclopedia.kids.net.au/page/in/Intelligence_agencies
A list of intelligence agencies by country, with links to each.

Publisher's note to educators and parents: Our editors have carefully reviewed these websites to ensure that they are suitable for students. Many websites change frequently, however, and we cannot guarantee that a site's future contents will continue to meet our high standards of quality and educational value. Be advised that students should be closely supervised whenever they access the Internet.

INDEX

A
Afghanistan 27, 28
al-Qaeda 27
assassinations 9, 26, 27
atomic bomb 20

B
bin Laden, Osama 27, 28
Blackwater 44
Border Patrol, U.S. 37

C
Castro, Fidel 23, 26
Central Intelligence Agency (CIA) 7, 9, 10, 25, 26, 27, 28, 29, 33, 42, 44
Clinton, Hillary 38, 41
Coats, Dan 11
Cold War 16, 18, 20, 21
Comey, James 40, 41
counterintelligence 5, 21
counter-terrorism 36, 37
crime 12, 37
Cuba 23, 26
cybercrime 30, 33, 34, 38

D
"deep state" 42, 43
Director of National Intelligence 10, 11
drugs 12, 37

E
enhanced interrogation 33
espionage 6, 14, 16–21, 34

F
fake news 38
Federal Bureau of Investigation (FBI) 4, 9, 10, 36, 40, 41, 42
foreign affairs 9, 11, 22, 24–29
France 8

G H
government, intelligence and 38–45
Greenhow, Rose O'Neal 15
Guantanamo Bay 31, 33
hacking 14, 19, 34, 38
Hari, Mata 15

I
intelligence agencies, US 10, 11, 12, 13
international law 9, 23, 25
Iran, coup 25, 26
Islamic State (ISIS) 22, 24, 29

J L
James Bond 16
legislation 45

M
MI5 8, 17
MI6 8
Middle East 22, 24
military intelligence, US 5, 8, 13, 22
Mossadegh, Mohammad 26
Mueller, Robert 42
Murphy, Richard and Cynthia 18

N
National Security Agency 11, 12
9/11 terror attacks 10, 27, 36
Northern Alliance 28

O P
Obama, Barack 19
presidential election (2016) 19, 38, 40, 42
propaganda 5, 22, 24

R
Rosenberg, Julius and Ethel 20
Russia 18, 19, 21, 29, 34, 40, 42

S
security, national 5, 30–37
spies 15, 16, 18
State Department, US 32
surveillance 6, 11, 12, 36, 37
Syria 29

T
Taliban 28
terrorism 5, 10, 27, 30, 33, 35, 36, 37
Travel Warnings 32
Trump, Donald J. 29, 38, 41, 42

U V
Ukraine 34
United Kingdom 8
USA PATRIOT Act 36, 37
Voice of America 24, 25